ABOUT THE AUTHOR

Luke Wright is a poet and broadcaster. His poetry stage shows have toured the world and played sold-out runs in London and Edinburgh. He is a regular contributor to BBC Radio and his verse documentary on Channel 4 was nominated for a Grierson Award. His first collection, *Mondeo Man*, was published in 2013.

PRAISE FOR FRANKIE VAH

'With *Frankie Vah*, he's managed to craft a gorgeously-worded powerhouse of a play, in one of the only verse dramas that could claim to get a crowd cheering and stamping their feet throughout. Again.'

★★★★★ *Broadway Baby*

'This is a mature, lyrical and politically relevant piece of poetic writing ... beautifully performed... I watched and listened in awe and pleasure, just drinking, drinking, drinking in the beauty of this show.'

★★★★★ *Exeunt*

'This isn't just socialist agit-prop, though; it reaches far further than that. In his visceral, virile verse, Wright skewers the essential cadences of all political drama.'

★★★★ *The Stage*

'[Wright] explores the themes that are central to our lives, the light and shade of lives lived to the full. He connects with all of us in a performance that feels so personal that it must be his own story, but this is theatre, this is telling a tale, this is poetry in motion, a ballad for right now.'

★★★★★ *Norwich Eye*

ALSO BY LUKE WRIGHT

POETRY

The Toll (Penned in the Margins, 2017)

Mondeo Man (Penned in the Margins, 2013)

The Vile Ascent Of Lucien Gore And What The People Did (Nasty Little Press, 2011)

High Performance (Nasty Little Press, 2009)

VERSE DRAMA

What I Learned from Johnny Bevan (Penned in the Margins, 2016)

NON-FICTION

Who Writes This Crap? with Joel Stickley (Penguin, 2007)

Frankie Vah

Luke Wright

Penned in the Margins

LONDON

PUBLISHED BY PENNED IN THE MARGINS
Toynbee Studios, 28 Commercial Street, London E1 6AB
www.pennedinthemargins.co.uk

The right of Luke Wright to be identified as the author of this work has been asserted
by him in accordance with Section 77 of the Copyright, Designs and Patent Act 1988.

First published 2018

Printed in the United Kingdom by TJ International

ISBN
978-1-908058-58-4

for Rosy

T HIS STORY STARTS at university.
Some people leave home ready, almost baked,
a diary full of hangovers and heartaches
stuffed inside their rucksacks. But not me.

I come from Dedham Vale. That bit of Essex
Constable painted. It hasn't changed
that much. An adolescence spent gazing
at ponds and water mills... and altar screens.

See, Dad's a vicar. Actual vicar. Yup.
I needed university. I tingled
at the thought. Three years to make myself.
And so... I joined loads of societies.

A desperate attempt to pour myself
into a score of moulds until I set.
From Buddhism to sailing via Urdu
and, my favourite one, creative writing.

Honey pot for nerds. We'd meet up in
the union once a fortnight and swap stories.
We went on socials too. And one of these
would change it all, would change it all forever.

It was in the Spring. A bar in town.
We'd heard a bunch of poets would be on.
Instead, we walked into a full-on gig.
The Clash was ringing from the speaker stack;

the floor was rank and sticky; and the poets?
Frontmen, centre stage without a band.
They spat out angry words like Gatling guns,
political and urgent: Thatcher, Reagan,

skinheads, fascists, nukes, the tabloid press.
The bedsit generation shouting back;
they pumped the cultural landscape full of lead
then kicked the casings at the baying crowd.

These were the Ranting Poets. A new breed
of wordsmith, forged from punk and now at war
in Thatcher's Britain, spitting stunning lines
that ping-ponged round your aching brain for days.

John Cooper Clarke, Attila the Stockbroker,
Linton Kwesi Johnson, Swells and Joolz.
The rhythmic sermons emanating from
their beery pulpits beat a path to me.

I know it's niche, it's not for everyone,
but we all have a thing that lights us up,
something that makes our insides sing with joy.
The girl who tastes a kind of truth in numbers,

native-tongue in sums. The boy who feels
his body billow at the beck of bass
and drums. And right there in that skuzzy boozer,
rapt in rat-a-tat, a singular

desire consumed me: *I wanna do that.*
And so I went to every Ranter's gig I could,
scribbling poems, dreaming of the night
I'd take the stage and bare my bloody soul.

I got my politics from poetry.
The Ranters lead me to a secret door
that opened on a wild, exotic garden
of subversive thought and socialism.

It was '81 and radicals
were fighting on two fronts in Tory Britain.
As well as kicking out at Thatcher's reign
the Labour Party raged in civil war.

It all came to a head one Sunday night,
the end of Freshers' Week, my second year;
my friends and I all gathered round the box
to swear and shout at Labour's Autumn conference.

Tony Benn and Denis Healey's battle
for Deputy Leader of the Party.
But more than that: the battle for the soul
of Labour. For the future of the Left.

And Healey wasn't it. Too '70s;
befuddled under caterpillar brows,
with all the pickled fug of portly aunts
on sherry-sodden Sunday afternoons.

No. No. For me and all my new comrades
the future looked like Tony. Tony Benn.
Democracy and power for the people!
When Tony spoke he filled a space in me

left empty since I spurned my father's God.
Yes, there it was, at last, at last — belief.
Belief in something bigger than myself.
The answers seemed so clear. We knew it all.

First Thatcher and her Yankee fascist clown,
all Milton Friedman market forces porn.
Next hollow men like Healey and his type
who claimed to be like us but had no fight.

Then us and Tony Benn and all those women
down at Greenham. Chained to one another.
Flesh and blood against the guns and bombs.
Let it be Benn. Let it be Benn. Let it.

I'll say this once. The votes have been counted three times, Tony Benn:
forty-nine point five seven four. Denis Healey: fifty point four two six …

NO! NO! NO! NO! NO! NO! We screamed and spat
and hurled salty abuse that made us sound
like burly union reps. A glass was smashed
as righteous anger swooped and dived and howled.

Injustice so bare-faced and undiluted
I could scarcely breathe. The air was thick
with smoke and booze and on the tiny screen
our hero jammed his tongue beneath his lip.

But did not hang his head. So nor did we,
but stored the moment in our hearts and drank

and marched and scrawled our fag-ash manifestos
late at night, convinced that we were right.

Yes, that was me: a fist-clenched, bloody mess
of socialism, poetry and beer;
light years from who my parents were, and glad.
My time at university swept by

in student marches, rallies, gigs and chants,
crowd-surfing on a surge of youthful brio,
guts and gurning glory, righteousness
and right-on, sweaty-swaggered verve until...

I fucked up my exams.

§

I SHOULD HAVE shrugged it off, or learned my lesson
and sat my exams the following year.
Instead, I came back home to Dedham Vale
where all that time spent making me unravelled.

I arrived home in time for the election.
'83. The darkest night in Labour's
history. I knew the worst might come.

The polls had been horrendous for us but,

you know: you hope. I watched it with my father.
I was used to sharing my despair
with friends. At shooting swearwords at the box.
The contrast at the vicarage was stark.

Each time that Dimbleby delivered me
bad news, my Dad, still in his dog collar,
would add to it by tutting at my woe.
The type to leave his Christian empathy

at work. He snuffled to himself in sarky
glee when Tony Benn lost Bristol East.
My hero — out of Parliament. This brave
and noble man rejected in the booth

and all my Dad could do was laugh. Fuck him!
Three weeks before I would have packed my bags,
remained true to the person I'd become.
Instead the fight just festered in my guts

and spread its sullen poison till I tumbled
back into depressive adolescence.
My friends would write and detail marches, jobs

and invitations I could barely read.

The postmarks on their envelopes enough
to cut me to my core: Newcastle, London,
Manchester and Brighton — distant lights.
Unanswered, soon their letters stopped arriving.

I wallowed, bed-ridden with defeat.
Boo-hoo, poor me. I hid my tragic self.
Back in my teenage bedroom, crying to
the songs that used to fill my heart with hope.

An office job in Colchester and Sunday
mornings on the front pew watching Dad.
A mutant teenage life: a grown man
straitjacketed in someone else's world.

The bloody mess of Orgreave passed me by;
where bolshy miners manned the picket lines,
and their wise wives stretched out bean stew, I sulked.
And took to work with me the chorus of

parental tuts that scored the news each night.
At home, I'd spare my Dad my sharp retorts.
I'd swallow them like Auntie Jacqueline's scones

then spend my work day retching them back up.

I never stood a chance, back home in shame,
against a man with God's authority.

§

I REALLY FELT like that was it: I'd peaked.
That university had been my lot.
Two pin-striped, forced-grin years dragged by.
And then, last year, a college mate of mine
invites me to his party. Grotty little
terraced student place near Layer Road.
I knew some other people going, so
I went. Regretted it the moment that
I got inside and slipped my headphones off.
The haunting battle cry of *What She Said*
replaced with Axel F. I longed to be
outside again with Moz's mutton croon,
the icy English summer nipping through
my Harrington, but pushed on past the throng
of haircuts, geeks and geezers searching for
a can of something cold to nip my nerves.

And then I heard her: "Hey, I like your coat."

I looked around and all I saw was hair:
a shock of messy ringlets. Red and brown.
Good. Fucking. Hair. But what I noticed next
were her Doc Martens. Good guys wear DMs.

"Oh cheers. Ta. Thanks. I like your cherry reds.
Only good guys wear DMs... and fascists.
Not that you're a fascist. I'm not a fascist.
I hate fascists." She giggled. "Yeah, they're dicks.
Well, seeing as you're not a fascist... Hi.
I'm Eve." She flashed a massive, wonky smile.

I looked at Eve and there I saw an ally;
an English accent in some far-flung airport,
Doc Martens in a sea of polished brogues.
Those nervy pangs that can go hand in hand
with trysts like this just gone. With foreheads almost
touching, Eve and I just talked and talked,
through cans of lager, rum 'n' Cokes and baggy joints.
She too was stuck at home, working shit jobs.
Unsure of where she trusted life to take her.

"I'd love to do my art full-time. You know,
get paid for it." She painted proper paintings:
rooms and rituals of the working class

in dark, rich oils that got down in your bones.
Eve whipped the world of art like I had whipped
the Tories back at college. *Rich twats with*
these video installations, shit... Graffiti?
Oh so gritty, yah... She went to Bedales.
It's Duran Duran on a fucking plinth...
No... no... my stuff is so unfashionable.
She laughed and bit a painted-stained finger nail.
"So go on, do a poem, Si. For me."
She goaded me until I shared a bit.
"I love it! You should do gigs. Yeah! You should."
And in that moment I just knew I would.
Right then, with Eve, it all seemed possible.

A litany of thinkers, bands and barbs.
The Bronski Beat, The Pogues and Billy Bragg
were bellowed, beer cans brandished, burps applauded,
parents railed against, and Thatcher, Howe and Lawson
roundly trashed. And as she trilled her bar
job into tales that made me giggle like
a kid, I found her dark, brown eyes and hid
within their gaze. Those eyes were huge, her lips
as well, her oil paint-stained fingers pressing
on my thigh. Oh! Everything about her
screamed me over. All of me screamed back

till we were upstairs tearing at each other,
a smoky funk of booze and pheromones;
the licking, pushing, pressing, pummelling,
euphoric, sweat-drenched clench to be as one.

And then, next morning, under vast blue skies,
I stumbled sore towards the country bus,
sniffing my fingers for a trace of her
and rubbing poppy bruises on my neck.
My inner life cracked open, gushing out.

§

AND AFTER THAT, it was all about Eve.
Each kiss breathed self-belief back into me,
as we laid plans to move away to London.
But first I had to tell my Dad some things.
I couldn't let it fester any more.

"... every dreary Sunday morning more,
more prayer and dust, more cloying Eucharist,
eyes to the floor, that subjugated burr."
I channelled my old fourth form drama teacher,
Mr Purvis, with his Dave Lee Travis
beard. He told us all to feel the words

before we said them. *Acting, Mortimer!*
"All that shit you'd serve us up at home.
What chance did I have against you and Him?
Years! All those years that I spent terrified.
Pretending to believe. Pretending, Dad.
I don't believe. I don't believe in God."
My father's face stared blankly back at me.
"There, there it is. At last, at last I've said it.
And to think I used to try and feel it,
screw my eyes up tight and really pray."
I spat the P. I let the vowel sound hang.
"Oh Dad, it always felt like fucking bullshit.
Why believe? Why would you want to?
To kneel to... that? A god so paranoid
he has to hear your every fucking thought.
Your God is like a supernatural Stasi!"
I was well pleased with that line, still am.
"You lecture us on empathy and love
and then you go and vote for Her: for Thatcher!
Communities are being smashed to Hell
and still you cross Her box. What kind of Christian
does that, Dad? If I had prayers I'd send
them to the miners, shipbuilders — if only
I had prayers. But my words aren't laments."
I'm really sorry for this next bit, guys.

I mean, truly I am, it's utter cringe:
"My words are bombs. And I intend to fucking
throw them."

The room fell silent. Low, white winter light
revealed the dust. I caught my breath, my tears.
Then Eve, my lovely Evie, took my arm.
My father grunted something, but we left
with backpacks on, two pairs of DMs, and
single fares to London in our hands.

§

HI, I'M SIMON MORTIMER. This poem is called 'Shambling' and it's about
being young and a bit of a fuck-up, but knowing, like, you're right.
It's dedicated to, um, Eve.

shambling
we're your factory seconds
been dragged up on old John Peel sessions

shambling
we're gobshites, we're lairy
Astley and Spandau — somebody spare me

shambling
distorted and off-key
splattered in Thatcherism — just get it off me

shambling
we're your unwanted thrift
the ring of the ringroads in angular riffs

shambling, shambling
fingers on fretboards
shambling, shambling
bum noted bar chords
the scratch in the record
the hiss of the tape
we are glorious, garrulous, gutsy mistakes

shambling
we're the wait for the giro
the Pernod and blacks
and the bile of the biro

shambling
smothered in capital's armpit
laid out on our landlady's
dead mother's carpets

shambling
we're the piss in your lager
a key down the side of
your brand new Corrado

shambling
we are dole queue afternoons
we're those songs that you hate
we're those songs without tunes

shambling, shambling
the rumble in the jumble
shambling, shambling
misquotes and fumbles
we're loose but we're learning
we're grinding our gears
see that future you're hoarding
it's ours, give it here

wake up England
it's grey and it's shit
it's red tops for breakfast
it's fascists and tits

wake up England

where is your lionheart?
it's burst and it's buried
in a discarded mineshaft

wake up England
calling all Maggie's children
who fashioned Jacuzzis
from old stagnant millponds

wake up England
no you're doing it wrong
you're brittle-snap plastic
like you're made in Hong Kong

shambling, shambling
we're not your sky-scrapered docklands
or your get-back-to-work schemes in East Riding's lost towns
we're not your canapés, we are not your Beaujolais run
we're not your MFI wardrobes, or your synthesised drums

shambling, shambling
shambling, shambling
shambling, shambling
shambling...

no, we're records and books
hearts full of ideas
with not enough sleep
and too many beers...

Cheers.

§

I'D SPENT TWO decades taking the world in,
bamboozled by a hundred different mobs,
each willing me to think and act like them.
But that night, in a dingy London club,
I kicked out at the world and left a mark.

They say there's nothing like it — being on stage.
But I think that's some bullshit actors say
to set themselves apart from you and me.
'Cos really I just felt what we all want:
to do something, and be good at it.

But one thing wasn't right. As I left the stage,
I winced to hear the compère say my name.
That's Simon Mortimer. It just so... nice.
The sort of name that dabbles, then gives up,

and takes a job in law. My legal name.

And so I gave myself another one.
And in it lies a happy afternoon
alone, of scribbling and crossing out.
The day after my first gig. A good day.
A caffeine swirl of hope and self-belief.

And sure, I've riffed a few creation myths;
how *Frankie* smacks of '50s rock 'n' roll
and *Vah* give out a hit of German punk.
Once claimed it meant *provocateur* in Norse.
But truthfully, the name is meaningless.

Three syllables I just thought sounded good
together. Later on that night, half-pissed
on rough Bulgarian Merlot, I told Eve,
"It isn't Simon Mortimer!" She smiled.
"It's good, my love. Drink up. To Frankie Vah!"

§

TWENTY-FIVE AND fucked on love;
a boozy, post-gig Friday night,
all huddled in some scuzzy pub

on Albert Street in Camden Town.
A group of kids we barely know,
prison roll-ups, scarves and hats,
and someone's got a wrap of speed,
so in the toilet me and Eve
take turns to dab the sticky stuff
and rub it on our senseless gums,
then choke it down with tepid beer
and shudder as it scuffs our tongues.

And then it's us, it's only us.
It's me and her, with London lying
there before us, ready now,
let's do this thing, let's raze this town.
We night-bus it to Belgrave Square.
Let's bring the class war over there!
We paw and pull each other's hair
and build an ever-after out of
spiel spooling ever faster,
dive-jump off the old Routemaster,
tumble cleaved, then on our arses,
sit-up sore and stupid-stare
the crisp white might of Belgrave Square,
that panzer-plated properness,
the nerve centre of old empire,

and loose our guts to fuck shit up,
so sit there racing on a wall
and stutter-spit on power and war
and make a plan for what we'll do
if sirens ever wailed through
our lilting, love-filled little life
'cos I won't fight love, I won't fight
we'll meet in Bow and fly by night
we'll meet in Bow and fly by night
we'll fly by night, it'll be all right
we'll fly, we'll fly, we'll fly, we'll fly, my love...

§

AND FLY WE DID. Still high at home, we gabbled
our love in blunt staccato sentences
and danced our legs down to the knees. I ranted
bits of verse while Eve laid out her dreams.

"They only hate my stuff 'cos they can't do it,
can't paint for shit and so they're spraying cardboard
boxes and calling it art. The lazy fucks.
It's naval gazing, Simon, me me me.

But art, *real* art, has got a duty to

reflect the world, or smash the world, do something
with the world that it exists in, right?
And *my* art's gonna do that... *I'm* gonna do that."

We whispered midnight secrets with our cheek bones
streaked in make-up, measured time in sex,
and jewelled our necks in bruises. Living on
a diet of crisps and lukewarm pints of tea,

surrounded by Eve's paintings. Streaks of oil
that captured bedsits, council house kitchens,
and boozers softly slumbering in clouds
of blue-tinged cigarette smoke. Serious.

When Eve picked up a brush she didn't fuck
about. She worked entranced by oil and light
for hours. For Eve and I, our work was war.
But when we stopped our life was levity,

a squirm of giggles under nylon sheets.
We'd drift to dreamless slumber cleaved together.
"Eve... you saved my life." She'd touch my cheek.
"I know... but now it's you and me... forever."

§

FOR ALL THE DRAUGHTS and unrelenting smells,
we were so happy with our scabby flat.
We looked out over chimney pots and tiles
as crooked as our teeth and owned the view.

Eve got a part-time job — the flower stall
at Borough Tube. Some nights, she'd come back home
face-flushed, arms full of withering bouquets
we'd swing around our heads like Morrissey.

While Eve was at the stall, I prowled the flat
like a caged lion, repeating vicious verses:
partisan, political and primed
to whip my comrades up into a froth.

I dreamed of being asked to do Red Wedge.
Paul Weller's pressure group of left-wing bands
and agitprop-y stand-ups. They played gigs
to raise awareness, cash and cultural props

for Labour. How I wished to join that gang!
I'd tinker with these dreams as teabags stewed.
Me, centre stage with Weller, arms aloft,
as legions hailed the fall of Mrs T.

And so I charmed my way on bills with bands
and hoped that it might lead me to my dreams.
A poem while The Wedding Present set up;
some verses while the drummer from The Pastels

checked his snare. I loved these jangly bands.
They called this scene 'c86', and I
resolved to be their Poet Laureate.
To make these frantic, urgent gigs my home.

§

ALL RIGHT. My name is Frankie Vah. This is for all of us left out in the
cold. It's dedicated to our great leader.

In ice-blue twinset, stiff and starchy
comes the frosty matriarchy.
Is it me, or is it parky?
Here comes Lady Winter.

The rich have ditched paternalism.
Back in fashion: MALNUTRITION.
Slash our taxes, fill our prisons,
no contrition, Winter

Gung-ho general scolds the ranks
as Bully Britain sends in tanks,
the champagne popped as young men sank.
GOTCHA GOTCHA GOTCHA

It makes one long for Edward Heath, so loveable and lardy.
Compared to Lady Winter, Ted was practically Keir Hardie.
When only a million were unemployed and the Met was not
     an army,
the winter of his discontent feels positively balmy.

Matron to her cabinet lackeys,
(bulbous noses, oily, craggy)
choke-chain chutzpah keeps them happy.
SIT! It's Lady Winter

DEREGULATE! DEREGULATE!
Nurse the city! Smash the state!
Wave Union flags at Royal fetes,
Dictator Lady Winter.

All double-speaking, icy-hearted;
frees the psychopathic market;
feeds it on the working classes,
laughing, laughing, laughing!

The lady's not for turning, but she's not for feeling neither —
a sci-fi supervillian by a really shitty writer.
With Milton Friedman's wanton greed and Reagan there to
        guide her,
the lady's back in town tonight... there's anthrax on the rider.

Cheered on by the fascist dailies,
more like Hitler than Disraeli.
Look! His grave! Let's have a cèilidh!
Gaily Lady Winter.

History — do your job, define her.
Right extremist, rank hardliner;
goose-step bobby, bloodied miner;
Orgreave, Lady Winter.

Still Lady Winter sits there with her thin malicious grin
and calls the folk opposing her the enemy within;
she robs you of your citizenship, she robs you of your skin.
The working class can rot until another war begins
and Winter needs more fodder so she tugs upon the strings
and whispers patriotic lies and offers up your limbs.
But I will stand and sing this song, though many ears are tin.
And hope that we can burst the bud and usher in the spring.

Cheers!

§

I CAME OFF STAGE, sweat-soaked and peeled
my jacket off. A tonic from the bar,
a sprinkle of my hip-flask gin and then
"Hey kid, you fookin' got something, you know?"
I thought he meant the gin. But he went on.
"So Lady Winter's Mrs Thatcher, yeah?"
"Ah, yeah." He smacked his hands together.
"A simile, eh kid? That's fookin' great.
It's great to see some Ranting poetry.
What happened to the Ranters? Johnny Clarke's
a fookin' smack head now. And no one's shouting.
It's like she's fookin' won. Know what I'm saying?"
I nodded meekly. "Petey Wise, you've probably
heard of me." The bloke was really full on.
Five foot nought with shiny well-bic-ed skull.
His lurcher-eyes avoiding mine, he shifted on
his feet, a sort of subtle skank, and sucked
a Marlboro Light between each lispy phrase.
"I look after The Midnight Shift. I know
you've heard of them." I had. Of course I had!
The Midnight Shift — Crown Princes of the current

crop of indie bands I saw week in
week out round Camden Town. I loved The Shift.
"We're looking for a tour support next month.
The lads have got this single out then and
we're gonna do a sort of Red Wedge thing.
Yeah, rock the vote, that kind of jazz, kiddo.
Who knows: perhaps she'll take us to the polls."

I almost puked, I almost kissed his shiny head.
"Um, yeah," I coughed. "I think. I'm sure. I'm free."
"All right then. Nice one, kiddo. Here's me card.
The money's shit but think of the exposure.
Besides, it's public service. No one's gonna
pay you, kid, to change the fookin' world."

§

THE SUNDAY NIGHT before I leave
and Eve and I in filthy sheets,
a mess of plates and ashtray mugs.
We spoon in stoned half-sleep

as London plays a symphony
of hacking buses, crowing cats

and shutters pulled down shop windows
that filters through our flat.

The Bowie poster on the wall,
the piles of clothes, the book-propped sash
that lets in May to mingle with
the smell of sex and hash;

and time like melting candle wax,
as evening softly calls in night,
and everything near holy
in the Riesling-yellow light.

A holdall and a flight case packed
with pants and shirts and homemade merch:
the chapbooks, badges, demo tapes.
I think of my Dad's church

and how my childhood's leagues from here
and further still from where I'll be
a month from now — *a month on tour.*
I feel Eve stroking me

and mumbling, "I'll miss you, Si."
I kiss her neck "I'll miss you, Eve."

Excited for the road ahead
but terrified to leave.

Afraid of what the space between
my love and I would do to us.
Afraid to see my dreams take shape...

§

BUT NEXT, I'm drinking lager back stage with The Midnight Shift.
You know, just hanging out with them. No big deal. 'Cept it is!
At first I'm really shitting it. But as the drink kicks in,
I find a banter foothold and the conversation sings.

There's Boz on bass and Rich on drums and Rob on lead guitar.
True, on their own the three of them wouldn't have got that far.
But they had Euey Sedgewick — block-headed, black-rim specs,
a brown-toothed grimace, gammy-leg and permanent death breath —

but, oh my God, can he pen tunes? These angry, gut-wrenched
        things
with complex, haunting melodies that seep through feedback din.
A gutter-snipe McCartney spitting lyrics like a gun
amid a rage of bleached guitars and trashy, shambled drums.

I fucking love The Midnight Shift. Have I mentioned that?
And we hit it off! They didn't think I was a twat.
What's more, I nailed my set that night. I punched the air, and roared
and walked off stage invincible, that hit of being adored.

§

AND THINGS HAD GONE exactly as Pete hoped.
She did call an election. June 11th.
Last night of the tour. He'd timed it spot on.
While scores of candidates appeared at doors
to prattle, promise, preen, perplex and purr,
his young blade's bristled broadsides from the stage
would slice the zeitgeist. Here was relevance
and Petey Wise, a child of punk, knew *that*
brought with it column inches, fame and cash.

Unlike the Red Wedge gigs I'd longed to be
a part of, this was not for charity.
He took an advert in the *NME*:
The Midnight Shift — On The Election Trail,
a dizzy month-long list of dates and then
(be still my beating heart!) + *Frankie Vah.*

I couldn't work Pete out. He had ten years on us,

which should have made him seem so grown-up.
But Petey gabbled like a kid on sweets
and acted as a sort of punching bag.
He didn't drink, but brewed insanely strong
espressos on a camping stove he carried
with him everywhere. His lispy boasts
filled every silent second in the van,
a bullet storm of caffeinated bullshit.

I used to go to school with Morrissey.
I fookin' named The Smiths.That's MY idea.
I weren't just AT the Lesser Free Trade Hall.
I booked the gig. I put Sid up, he shat the bed.
He fookin' did. Anita Pallenburg?
Shagged her. Did! She knows me brother, Kevin.

If Petey hadn't done it, Kevin had.
Me brother, Kevin, used to play the drums
in Joy Division. He wrote half their tunes.
Me brother, Kevin, glassed a swan, bummed an 'orse,
played backwards bass on 'You can call me Al.'
Me brother, Kevin, does Glen Matlock's gutters.
He always said *Me brother, Kevin.* Not
just *Kevin* or *Me brother.* But *Me brother, Kevin.*
Pissed one night, Boz, Rob and I slapped Kevin

on the end of every phrase till tears
ran down our faces. "Best bit is," Boz wheezed,
"he's only got one brother. KEVIN! KEVIN! KEVIN!"

§

TWENTY-FIVE AND fucked on tour,
war paint on, then through the stage door
to amp stacks, call sheets, backstage pits
where green rooms stink of piss and shit.
The soundcheck, merch stall, half-arsed rider.
What the fuck Pete? Fuckin' cider.
Walls daubed in bad band names —
all the gold of third-rate fame
and people came, yes people came.

In toilet venues, ringroad pubs
and dole-age working people's clubs,
I ranted words above the hum
of pissed-up punters, line-check drums,
and saw my conscious cannonade
make burly bastards hush a mate
or stop a girl mid-swig to laugh.
My pulpit high above their hearts;
my congregation here at last.

And every day we heard the news;
then every night we spat abuse
at Thatcher and her Tory hoards.
As they campaigned from shore to shore
with thin-lipped smiles and Union Flags
we did the same with bottles, fags
and snarling, hard-edged metric lines;
there, centre-stage among my kind.
This is our time, this is our time,
this is *my* time.

§

— Eve, Eve, it's Frankie.
— Frankie?
— Huh? Sorry, Si. It's just... they all call me Frankie.
— How's it going?
— Amazing. Amazing. I'm selling loads of merch and people are listening... Fuck off Boz. Nah, fuck off. Sorry, look, I gotta go.
— Already?
— Sorry.
— I sold a painting, Simon.
— Amazing. That's great, well done.
— Yeah, it was...
— Boz... Fuck off... Fuck. Sorry love, I gotta go. I'll call you back.

§

EUEY AND I agree on everything.
An acquiescence loud as argument.
It's great to have it out with him. Back in
his hotel room we drain the rum and rant.
I'm used to Evie stopping me by now.
For God's sake Si, I know! You've said that twice.
Tonight, we say it all, at least four times.
Euey's on his feet and prowling mid-flow.
"Yeah, I love Tony Benn, 'n' all. I don't
remember '81, I were a nipper.
Fook me, turn it up." He cranks the telly.

Neil Kinnock, walking with his wife,
as stirring music surges. "This is it!"
he cries. "They're calling it Kinnock the movie!"
We watch, slack-jawed in drunken disbelief
at Labour's latest broadcast. Nine minutes
of schmaltzy orchestra and party grandees
blowing smoke up Kinnock's ginger arse.
When Healey chips in with his yucky smile
and says he's just like Gorbachev, we howl.
"Oh yeah, 'cos that'll win the middle ground,
you useless twats." The horror movie score

that creeps beneath the speech when Kinnock kicked
out Militant just seals the deal for us.
"You what mate?" Euey cries "They're our comrades,
they're not Darth Vader. Jeez." He turns it off.
Our first instinct's to sit and take the piss
but slowly all the banter drains away.
"They want to look all slick like Maggie, don't they?"
Euey says. "I know! It makes you think
what else will Labour do to get elected?
Privatise? Go nuclear? Perhaps
we'd all be better off to lose and hold
our heads up high." At this he laughs at me.
"I think you've had too much! Neil Kinnock's
just a ginger bollocks. But he's ours.
You'd rather him than Thatcher, right?" I nod.
"Of course. Of course. It's just well, I dunno."
But in my head I'm not so sure. Why should
we compromise? Fuck winning if it isn't
on our terms. I need... I need a cause
that I can boast about, a cause that's right
and pure. I need to get behind a cause
that makes my senses roar.

§

UP THE WEST COAST, down the east.
Through Stoke and Bradford, Hull and Leeds.
Front cover of the NME.
KICK OUT THATCHER Sedgewick pleads
and inside there's a bit on me.
NEW FACE OF RANTING POETRY.
There's an extract from 'Shambling'.
Mics feedback and Les Pauls ring.
I throw up in a motel sink.
I make can bongs and knock back gin
then in the splitter feeling grim,
midday — let the drinks begin.
Newcastle, Durham, Darlington.
I knock the same set out again,
the rat-a-tat machine gun shout,
election clock is timing out,
this one's about...

     this one's about...

        this one's about...

           this one's about

           §

"SIMON, YOU'RE NOT even listening."
We're back in London for one night only.
A sold-out gig in Camden. Everyone
is coming down. And I mean, everyone.
We heard a rumour Johnny Marr might come.
I'm in the tired dressing room with Eve.
We haven't seen each other in three weeks.
But mate, it feels like years. When she arrived
our hug was weird; she tried to snog me but,
self-conscious of my boozy breath, I went
to kiss her cheek. We dance around each other —
trodden toes and tense apologies.
"Sorry... Love... I'm trying to write this thing."
"It's a big deal for me this, Si. I sold
a painting." Evie puts her hand on my
shoulder. I want to shrug it off but don't.
"I'm proud of you," I say, not feeling it.
I look up and her huge brown eyes are wet.
"We'll celebrate it properly tonight,"
I manage. "When I've done my set, eh love?"
She shrugs. "All right. I gotta go now though.
I said I'd help out on the stall today."
"Uh-huh." The poem swallows me again.
Her hand is on the door. I stop myself.
"Eve. Wait. I really am sorry. We'll have

some fun tonight. Just you and me." She smiles.
"All right, I love you, Si."

                              "I love you too."

                    §

THIS ONE'S ABOUT Neil Kinnock's move into Hollywood.

  I used to cringe at soppy lefties
  linking hands at conference time;
  that awkward mono-tonal dirge
  to *Keep The Red Flag Flying High.*

  Despair! Despair! My face in my hands
  at Michael Foot's sartorial whims.
  No wonder all those banners kept on
  falling down on him.

  Yes, I was all in favour of
  assuring folk that we were able:
  NO to falling in the sea
  and NO to tripping over tables.

  Ironed shirts and tied-up ties
  don't make you the Gestapo.

I'm all for being Marxist mate,
but let's be Karl not Harpo.

We needn't look like Übermensch,
we needn't look like Kevin Klein,
but let's look like we're in Government
and not *Last of the Summer Wine.*

That wisdom made some sense to me,
the need to cast a wider net.
We even let them muzzle Benn
and look at what we bloody get.

Neil Kinnock on a clifftop.
Someone spare me please.
My party went to an ad man
and all I got was this lousy cheese.

Wheezy, greasy party grandees
coax, cajole and cough.
Wheel on Healey! What's that Den?
He's just like Gorbachev?

Well, that'll bag the middle ground,
you creepy grinning nobhead.

Watch it Den, two caterpillars
trying to eat your forehead.

The first Kinnock in a thousand years
to go to Hollywood;
the problem is the film of his
just isn't any good.

Those sweeping, weeping violins.
Christ, where's the fight and fizz?
It's like you're trying to sell me something.
I just don't what it is.

So give me pratfalls, donkey jackets
lengthy suicide notes.
Let's mobilise the dispossessed
and not chase Tory votes.

§

OFF STAGE, and Eve is there. "You watch yourself.
I think that Kinnock one pissed people off."
"Nah, it's all right," I laugh. "I'm joking. Look,
I've gotta go and flog some merch now, but
I'll be right back." She smiles. I think she smiles.

I lead a merry band of punters to
the stall and pop my case. I'm flogging tapes
and photocopied chapbooks of my stuff.
I'm signing too. I've changed my signature.
The pigeon scrawl that used to sign my cheques
has gone, big spiky letters thrust across
the title page and inlay of the tapes.
"Can you sign this one for my son? For Johnny."
"All right." She nods. "He loves your stuff."
"How old is he?"

                              "He's ten." Huh? What the fuck?
"He's ten! How does he even know my stuff?"
"He's seen you in the *NME*!" she tuts.
"He's very clever, Johnny, mark my words,
he wants to be a poet, just like you."
I beam and sign her book. "So what's your name?"
"I'm Sandra," she replies with grass-green eyes
that seem to ache and sparkle all at once.
We're holding up the queue. She smiles and leaves.
Then next, a bloke, perhaps a bit older
than me. His work suit on, tie poking from
a trouser pocket. "Yeah. Good set that, mate.
But Kinnock's all right. Gonna vote for him."
I go to make a joke, he cuts me off.
"I voted Tory last time. Labour was

a mess, but he's all right. Good bloke." I stare
at him. "You voted fucking Tory! What?"
I couldn't believe he was at our gig.
"I weren't the only one!" The bloke grins back.
I shove a book unsigned into his hand
and carry on until I'm out of merch.
Then Eve is there. "Is it always like that?"
"What, Tory Boy? No, can't believe it really."
"What?" she says. "No, Si, I meant that girl.
You practically got off with her!" I put
my merch case down. "You fucking what?"
"You, flirting with your fucking groupie, Si!
Is this what it's like in your fucking boys' club?
Men do all the talking, while girls clap
and fawn all over you. I bet it is."
I'm lost for words, she's being such a dick.
"You haven't even asked about my painting."
"Oh! Your painting, Eve! What about it?"
But as I say the words, The Midnight Shift
meander on to stage. The cheers ring out.
Rich bangs his sticks. Eve shoots this ugly look
at me but then we're lost in chords and crowds.
The atmosphere is nigh-on nuclear.
Each note a cry of fury from the Gods.
I'm knocked for six and when I clock back in

Eve's gone. I look around for her, but all
I see are sweaty girls and boys, arms raised
and thrashing to the music. Euey snarls
and everyone snarls back. And I think *fuck her.*
Fuck. I dab some speed, and then some more:
the gig becomes a backstage bomb, and then
a club, and then a den as London bleeds
the orange blur of taxi lights, the neon
pink of Soho clubs, it smears across
my consciousness, I want to have it all.
Fuck her, fuck that, fuck it, 'cos I'm all right.
I fill my throat and aching lungs and roar
into the night.

§

I WAKE UP some place I don't know,
a vomit smell and all alone.
No time to get to Eve and so
it's in the splitter, off we go
and back up North for six more shows.
Now everything is drab and slow
and Labour's slipping in the polls;
the sky is muck, the chevrons roll;
despair and nausea take ahold;

reflected in the toilet bowl,
the liquid lunchtime of the soul.
I'll take the desk, I'll take the dole.
Just anything to get me home;
away from Petey's caffeine drone,
from plastic food in styrofoam.
The grey macadam's in my bone.
Oh Evie, please pick up the phone...
Oh Evie, please pick up the phone.
I fumble for the words I wrote.
My punchlines wither in my throat;
at sea in drink and scarce afloat
my poems shrink, my intros bloat,
the lines emerge from desperate gropes,
I never did my postal vote,
the punter's trust in me just goes,
hotels and roads, hotels and roads,
and Petey's in my face like strobes,
an endless epileptic probe,
Sort it out, kid. Drink alone.
I drink alone, I drink alone
until there's just one show to go.
In Ipswich too, ten miles from home.
I think of Dad and feel so low.
We haven't said a word since... fuck.

No get on stage Si, drink it up,
election night! The crowd go nuts.
Maggie, Maggie, Maggie. Out, out, out!
I writhe and rant and fist and pout
in sweet applause and bolshy shouts;
it rains on me, I drink it down,
I drink it down.

§

I'M THERE, in white lights, white noise hum, backscatter on my
          vision,
a Rizla bomb of sweat and bile. I grip the shaky mic stand

and battle with the half-pissed crowd, a dance of flirt and fight.
They tune back in to clap and roar at anti-Tory stuff.

Two women by the speaker stack are giving me the eye.
One looks a bit like Eve; a shock of curls, a massive smile.

I rant out 'Lady Winter', though I stumble through the ending,
and as the clapping's calming down some fella shouts out: *Kinnock!*

And in that moment, something snaps. I've done my Kinnock bit.
I've told them what I fucking think. He's trying to start some shit.

My heart is open in my chest, inside's a half-formed rant,
and next my heart is on my sleeve and everything is pouring out.

I used blame the Tories, mate, more recently blamed Kinnock,
but when you think of it, they're not the ones that drop us in it.
You get the government you deserve and YOU deserve this lot
and if you need convincing, well, then you deserve to rot.

The answer's fucking obvious! Can't see it, then you're thick.
Oh, we need Euey Sedgewick to spoon feed us this shit.
We'll only vote for Labour if you put a fucking gig on.
What's the matter, don't like truth? Keep your fucking wig on.

You turn up every five years, cross your box and then go home and
think the world will fucking change for you. Well, let me tell you
now: it fucking won't. This is all your fault. The fact that you won't
tune to politics unless it's made cool by a fucking band — it says it
all. Yeah fucking boo me then, fuck you fuck you fuck...

More follows but it's drowned out by the crowd.
And who can blame them? They're not here for this.
Election night, they want to feel good.
I don't even believe the things I'm saying,
slurring pissed-up bilge. I try to start
another poem; more boos come and then

a bottle hurls towards me, hits my chest.
I'm soaked, I drop the mic and just stand there.
The noise that comes is low and menacing;
I've given them a licence to loathe me.
And every traffic jam, each argument,
each cup of tea gone cold, each bad night's sleep,
or dog turd trodden in or slick MP
whose lies they've had to sit and listen to
is channelled in the jeers they throw at me.
The venom I encourage them to spit
at Thatcher and the other bogeymen
I aim my poems at, now comes for me.
My cheeks begin to smart. I'm going to cry.
I run off stage and into Petey Wise.
"You eejit Frank, they'll trash the amps.
We gotta get the fookin' band on now,"
he says to nobody and everyone.
The band trudge past. "You fookin' dick," Boz says.
Euey just shakes his head at me. "Too much!"
The room's a blur. I flop down on a chair;
behind me chords and drums bleed from the stage.
The threat of riot must have passed 'cos Petey's
back and right up in my face. "You child.
You fookin' child... I'll tell you this for nowt:
you're just so fookin' wrong about it all.

He's all right, Neil Kinnock, people like him.
You're not supposed to like that film. It ain't
for you. To win you've got to govern for
old Tories like your Dad, and Trots like you.
I know you think I'm just a chancer, Frank.
But fook you, kid, I care. Me brother, Kevin,
and me grew up with fookin' nowt because
of Tory scum. So fook your principles.
I wanna win." I try to bat him off.
"You're just a fucking Tory, Pete," I slur.
The look he shoots at me is utter dirt.
"It ain't about you, kid. That's socialism."
I haven't got an answer. Words are slow.
The certainty I felt in Euey's room
the week before is fading now. I just...
I just need something I can believe in,
to feel that rush, that hit of certainty.
And then I see her, by the back door. Eve.
No wait ... it's her, that girl from the front row.
I stumble off the chair and push past Pete.

§

AND NOW IT's me and her, we've got a bottle,
sitting on the steps around the back.

She liked my set. I fish for compliments
and bathe in all her giggled, gushing praise.
I sense my self-belief begin to build.
The vodka burns my throat. I feel the bass
and bass drum in my guts. My eye's a lens:
it clocks the dirty tarmac of road,
her DMs grinding out a fag, her tights,
a neon purple pulled around the thick
curve of her calf. I touch the shiny boot.
I like your boots. I feel her ankle through
the buffed black leather, let my fingers slide
across its shine, then past the lip and now
the nylon of her tights. A sharp intake
of breath, her hand is on my knee and moving
up my thigh. The face is unfamiliar.
No... No turning back. The earth subsides
beneath me and I slide, falling apart,
until she's lying down across the steps
her skirt pushed up and I'm on top of her.
The thinness of her vodka breath, her breasts
against my beating chest, my bricks dislodge
and tumble down, collapsing as we kiss;
yes, I think, I can believe in this.
Right now, I can believe in this. I can
believe in this.

§

I DON'T KNOW how long Eve was standing there.
She never said a word. I just looked up.
Her face was... Trying to pull my jeans back up.
I ran after her, back into the club.
The way she looked at me. Like she was scared.
I grasp for words. What words? My words are bombs.
She just said: "You had me to believe in."

She'd come down with my Dad. A big surprise.
She wanted him to see my set, to see
me *triumph*, she'd said. And they'd seen it all.
My Dad was standing stiffly at the door.
My gaze met his, he turned away. They left.
I knew he'd take her to the vicarage.
My home. I knew I wasn't welcome there.

§

AND THAT WAS just last night. I woke up at
a bus shelter with vomit down my T-shirt.
I'm at my parents' now, but Eve's long gone.
My father sits across his desk from me.
He doesn't speak. The nausea washes through me.

"Well," he says at last, "you've blown it there.
That poor girl, Simon. What on earth were you..."
We stare each other down. Why am I here?
"So that was why you left, was it? To get
on stage and scream expletives at people?"

I've can't do this with him."Fuck you!" I spit.
I go to leave. "Yes, run away, Simon.
Go blame the world. It's always someone else's
fault. It's mine, or God's, or Margaret Thatcher's.
Never yours." I bite my lip and turn.

"All right, I fucked up, Dad. I fucked it up."
He winces at the swearwords. Good. It shores
me up. I tell myself: *I will not cry.*
"You happy now? Got what you wanted, Dad?"
He tries to speak, I cut him off. "Just don't.
I've had a fucking lifetime of your sermons.
Save it for your parishioners. Your sheep."

He stares at me. "Is that what you were doing?
Thinking for yourself? My goodness, Simon.
You got obsessed with politics until
you mucked up your degree. You wallowed in
your misery until you lost your friends.

You chucked your family in for Eve, and now
you've chucked her in! For what? I mean, for what?"

The nausea's leaving tide marks ever higher.

"I understand. You don't believe in God.
I'm fine with your decisions. I admire
you for finding something else to put
your faith in but... you can't just hitch a ride
on people or ideas then drop them when
the going gets too tough. To love something
and place your faith in it can be euphoric.
I know that feeling, Simon, all too well."

"You don't," I shout. "How could you fucking know?"

"I know... because I used to be like you.
Obsessed with my beliefs, addicted to
the way they made me feel. I blew it too.
I pushed the ones I loved away when they
cast doubt on my beliefs. It took me years
to learn to compromise. I'm still not good
at it. You know that much. Don't be like me.
Don't throw it all away when you are tested.
Euphoria and doubt go hand in hand.

See it through, make compromises with..."

"No," I say. "I don't want to compromise."

"But that is how we learn! It's how we add
a depth to everything we understand.
It's how we get to empathy and love."
He loosens his dog-collar as he talks.
"Don't chase your beliefs; let them live in you.
You needn't run away from everyone
to be the man you feel compelled to be."
The room is underwater, but Dad smiles.
He lets me cry as minutes pass us by.

"And I suppose you'll need somewhere to stay."
I falter here. My eye is drawn towards
the headline of the paper on his desk.
Thatcher Sweeps Back to Number Ten. A picture
of the Iron Lady's thin-lipped smile.
Majority expected to be more
than one hundred. "No. No, it's all right, Dad,
I need to give myself another go."
He nods. And then we hug. At first it's strange;
I can't recall the last time that we did.
But now I'm clinging on to him and him

to me. And everything comes out. I sob
for him and Mum and Petey, Euey, Boz
and all the band. But most of all for Eve.
Oh, Eve. I sob. The pain is coursing through
my body, white and savage, burning hard.
And with each sob my father grips me tight.
"She's gone, my boy, she's gone, she's gone, they've gone."

And now I'm out the door with salty cheeks.
My hangover's a hand around my throat.
It's gonna hurt tonight. It's gonna hurt
for months and months and months, but I will face it.
Nothing's certain now; I think that's right.
I have to hold my own: euphoria
and doubt, and maybe even compromise.
In time the bud will burst, and when it does
I'll be ready for the spring.

THANKS

Frankie Vah was commissioned by Paul Jellis, Soho Theatre and Norfolk & Norwich Festival. It debuted at Norwich Playhouse as part of the 2017 Norfolk & Norwich Festival, and completed a full run at The Underbelly during the Edinburgh Festival Fringe 2017, produced by Underbelly Productions and Paul Jellis. Thanks are due to William Galinksy, David Luff and Steve Marmion, who believed enough in my idea to give me some money to make it.

The production was worked on by Steve Forster, who talked me up to the press; Ian Catskilkin, who composed the visceral, *Wedding Present*-esque score; Tom Clutterbuck, who designed visuals and lights; Joe 'Lamps' Price, who did further lighting design; Kerri Charles, who stage managed the show in Edinburgh and put up with my shit; Martha Rose Wilson, who was Assistant Producer and one day will rule the world; and Tara Wilkinson, who raided the Underbelly's vaults to make sure we all got paid.

John Cooper Clarke, Phill Jupitus and Ian McMillan all gave up their time to star in a trailer for the show. See those guys, I love those guys!

Thanks are also due to Martin Rowson for filling me in on the sort of thing Eve might have railed against; Neil Lawson for answering questions about the 1987 election; and, especially, Attila The Stockbroker, for answering my questions and inspiring me to be a proto-ranter all those years ago.

Joe Murphy and Alex Thorpe co-directed the production. Joe provided lots of early edits and helped shape the narrative. Alex and I spent many happy hours in a rehearsal room at the fabulous Fisher Theatre in Bungay shaping the text and eating the excellent sandwiches from the Earsham Street Deli. Thank you both, from the bottom of my mushy pink heart. We made this.

Thanks to Tom Chivers for agreeing to commit this to paper. My continued membership of Penned in the Margins' stable is an honour and a pleasure. And thanks in advance to James Trevelyn for sharing this story far and wide.

Personal thanks are due to my incredible family: Rosy, Aidan, Sam and Olive.

Finally, special thanks are due to Paul Jellis, who commissioned, produced and believed in this story from day one. The mind of a scholar and the palette of a gentleman. And like me, he doesn't know when to go to bed.